We Celebrate
New Year

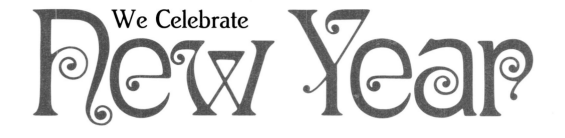

Bobbie Kalman   **Tina Holdcroft**

The Holidays & Festivals Series

Crabtree Publishing Company

The Holidays and Festivals Series
Created by Bobbie Kalman

Writing team:
Bobbie Kalman
Susan Hughes
Kathleen Smith

Illustrations:
Tina Holdcroft
© Crabtree Publishing Company

Editor-in-chief:
Bobbie Kalman

Editors:
Susan Hughes
Lise Gunby
Grace DeLottinville
Dan Liebman

Research:
Lise Gunby
Cathy Cronin

Cover design:
Peter Maher, Newton Frank Arthur Inc.
Karen Harrison

Art direction and design:
Jane Hamilton
Hugh Michaelson
Catherine Johnston

Mechanicals:
Nancy Cook

For Beverly

350 Fifth Ave., Suite 3308
New York, N.Y. 10118

360 York Road, R.R.4
Niagara-on-the-Lake, Ontario L0S 1J0

73 Lime Walk
Headington, Oxford OX3 7AD

Cataloguing in Publication Data
Kalman, Bobbie, 1947-
  We celebrate New Year

(The Holidays and festivals series)
Includes index.
ISBN 0-86505-041-4

1. New Year. I. Title. II. Series.

GT4905.K35 1985   398.2'683   LC93-27355

Contents

It's almost here!

It is five minutes before midnight. A huge crowd of people has gathered. In a few minutes it will be time to say good-bye to the old year.

We remember the fun we had in the old year. What will the next year bring? All kinds of new and exciting things will happen to us. We are sorry to see the old year end. It has been like a friend. At the same time, we look forward to the unknown experiences of the new year.

4

The crowd is buzzing with excitement now. Ten . . . nine . . . eight . . .
seven . . . six . . . five . . . four . . . three . . . two . . . one . . .

5

New beginnings

When does a new year begin? It can begin at different times.
The beginning of something special can be thought of as a new year.
The start of a marriage or a friendship can mark a new year in a person's
life. When you start a new grade in school, you are beginning a new school
year. When you celebrate your eighth birthday, you are starting a new
year of life, your ninth year.

6

For thousands of years, people celebrated the new year in springtime. In the spring, the flowers bloom and the branches of the trees sprout tiny green leaves. Nature comes to life again after the winter.

People in some countries still celebrate the new year in the spring. In Iran, there are four New Year's Days every year. People celebrate the beginning of each of the seasons.

Perhaps you celebrate January 1 as New Year's Day. Many people celebrate the beginning of a calendar year. January is the first month of our calendar.

Caesar's calendar

Julius Caesar lived two thousand years ago. He was a great Roman ruler. He decided to change the Roman calendar so that each year would have twelve months. The first month of the year was named Januarius after the Roman god, Janus. People thought that Janus had two faces. One face looked backward and the other looked forward. In the month of Januarius, people looked back over the past year and ahead to the next year. The month of Januarius became a good time to celebrate a new year. Now Januarius is called January.

Sun and moon

Julius Caesar created a special calendar for the Romans. Other countries also made their own special calendars. The first month of a calendar may not be January. Some calendars are called *lunar* calendars. They are based on the movement of the moon. Some calendars are based on the movement of the earth around the sun. These calendars are called *solar* calendars. The calendar that most people follow is the Gregorian calendar. It is based on the sun and the moon.

The Chinese celebrate the New Year when they see the second new moon in the sky after December 22. The second new moon usually rises between the middle of January and the middle of February. The Jewish calendar is also a lunar calendar. The first day of the Jewish calendar year usually comes at the end of the summer or at the beginning of the autumn. Each month in the Muslim calendar begins at the time of the new moon. The Muslim calendar does not have 365 days in its year as our calendar does. The Muslim New Year can occur in different seasons.

Whenever you celebrate New Year's Day, it marks the beginning of a new time. Read about all kinds of New Year celebrations. Think of the different ways you might want to celebrate New Year.

Time to take over!

Old Year yawned. He reached over and turned off his alarm clock. He yawned again. Slowly his eyes closed. Old Year fell back to sleep. He began to snore. "Hrrumpph!" he awoke with a start. Slowly, he sat up in bed. "Oh, I'm sooooo tired," Old Year muttered. Carefully, he got out of bed. "My poor back," he sighed. "My poor legs. My poor sore feet. My aching head."

Old Year was glad that today was his last day of work. New Year would spend the day with him learning the duties of the job. Then New Year would take over and Old Year could enjoy a well-deserved rest. "Well-deserved indeed," Old Year groaned to himself.

There was a tap at the door. In came New Year. Old Year was shocked at how young New Year looked. "Why, you're only a baby," he said. "Do you think you can handle a full-time job such as this one?" New Year shrugged his shoulders. "I don't want the job," he sneered. "You can keep it." He turned around and started back out the door.

"Who cares?"

Old Year jumped up as quickly as his old bones would let him. "Now, you wait a minute, you young whippersnapper," he called. "You just wait a minute. Let's talk this over." New Year stopped and turned. He shrugged his shoulders again. "Nothing to talk about," he said. "I don't want the job."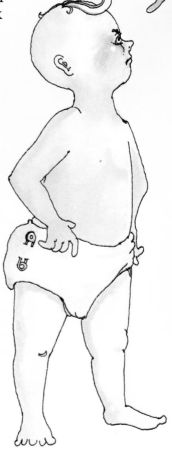

"But I'm too old to do it anymore," Old Year insisted. "There must be a New Year to carry on. Why, if you don't take this job, there is no one else who can. What will happen to the people of the world?" Old Year was puffing after this long speech. He lowered himself into a chair and looked anxiously at New Year.

"Who cares?" said New Year. He shrugged his shoulders, folded his arms, and put a big pink pacifier in his mouth.

Old Year could not believe his ears or his eyes. "Who cares?" he shouted. He jumped up out of his chair. "Come with me," he said, and grabbed New Year by the hand. "We're going on a trip." Off they went.

8

Around the world

The first stop was India. "Do you see all these lights?" Old Year asked New Year. Small lamps covered the roofs of all the houses. "These lights are welcoming *you*." The next stop was Japan. Children were making lucky decorations. Old Year pointed his finger. "These pine, bamboo, and rope decorations are welcoming *you*, New Year."

In Portugal, New Year heard the children sing songs to him. He heard the bells in Hungary ringing for him. He saw the people in the Philippines wearing their best clothes for him. In the United States and Canada, people were busy preparing for parties in his honor. Around the world, people were looking forward to meeting and greeting New Year.

Finally, the tour was over. "Well?" puffed Old Year as he sank into his chair, exhausted. "Now do you care what happens to the people of the world?"

New Year's promise

New Year nodded his head once, twice, three times. "Yes," he said. "Oh, yes. I did not realize how important this job was. I did not know how friendly the people of the world were. I did not know how much they really needed me. I will make a promise for the new year. I will meet each person. I will visit every home and say, "New Year is here, just for you. I will . . .""

New Year talked on excitedly. He was full of plans for his new job. He wanted to be the best New Year the people of the world had ever welcomed. New Year was so excited, he did not see Old Year close his eyes, stretch his arms, and yawn. He did not see Old Year sink even deeper into his chair and, with a smile on his lips, say, "Happy New Year." And he did not hear Old Year begin to snore — softly!

9

Tallying up the old year

Many people like to say good-bye to the old year by remembering what kind of year it has been. They ask themselves questions. Was it a happy year? What were the happiest things that happened? What were the saddest things that happened? This is called tallying up. Some people write down the answers to these questions. These are their memories of the old year.

How do you say good-bye to the old year? Try playing this game. It will help you remember what kind of a year you have had.

Sit down with a pencil and a piece of paper. Give yourself a starting score of 30. Read each item listed below. If it applies to you in the past year, you must take the points beside it. If the item does not apply to you, go on to the next line. The numbers in the first section are *added* to your score. The numbers in the second section must be *subtracted*.

Points to be added

+ 3 did not miss any school
+ 3 told parents or teacher the truth about something you did, knowing you might be punished
+ 3 helped a friend with homework
+ 3 made a sad friend feel better
+ 3 visited a sick friend
+ 2 read this book and liked it
+ 2 did household chores without being asked
+ 2 looked after a younger child without being paid
+ 2 discussed problem instead of fighting
+ 2 made a new friend
+ 1 shared lunch
+ 1 wrote a card or letter to a grandparent or other adult relative
+ 1 offered to help the teacher
+ 1 shared your best toy with a friend
+ 1 treated a parent to breakfast in bed

Points to be subtracted

- 3 did not return library books
- 3 had three desserts after a meal
- 3 rode a bicycle down the wrong side of the road
- 3 crossed the street without going to the crosswalk
- 3 left room looking like an obstacle course
- 2 returned library books with dog-eared pages or with cards missing
- 2 returned library books late
- 2 did not look both ways when crossing the street
- 2 made a fuss at bedtime
- 2 did not brush teeth at bedtime
- 1 ate pickles for breakfast
- 1 put too much sugar on breakfast cereal
- 1 did not come when parents called
- 1 turned bedroom light back on after parents left the room
- 1 did not put toys away

How did you score?

55-60 points	If your score is this high, you don't need to make any New Year's resolutions!
45-54 points	You have had a very good year. Congratulations!
37-44 points	Keep up the good work.
25-36 points	Work on getting more bonus points next year.
18-24 points	Much improvement needed.
10-17 points	You can do better than this.
0-9 points	I hope your next year is better!

Ways of welcome

After saying good-bye to the old year, people welcome the new year with celebrations. The people in this picture greet the new year in different ways. You will find out more about these customs as you read this book. Match the numbered pictures to these countries and customs:

A. Greece — ''eating in'' the new year

B. Spain — ''popping in'' the new year

C. Canada — ''ringing in'' the new year

D. England, Denmark — ''throwing in'' the new year

E. Laos — ''splashing in'' the new year

F. Wales — ''mumming in'' the new year

G. Bahamas — ''junkanooing in'' the new year

H. India — ''lighting in'' the new year

I. Japan — ''writing in'' the new year

J. Israel — ''blowing in'' the new year

Answers:
A - 6; B - 10; C - 1; D - 7; E - 3; F - 8; G - 5; H - 4; I - 9; J - 2.

Ringing in the new year

Ring out the old, ring in the new,
Happy bells ring fast and slow.
The year is going, let him go,
Ring out the old, ring in the new.

In many parts of the world, people ring bells to announce that the new year has come. The following story rings with the sounds of bells. Can you spot the hidden bell sounds? They are ding, ting, ring, bel, and bell. Bal is another bell sound. For example, *bal*cony sounds like *bell*cony. Look for the hidden sounds at the beginning and the end of each word in the story. For example, there is a ''ring'' in the word ''string'' and a ''ding'' in the word ''wedding.'' Some words with bell sounds are repeated and must be counted each time they occur in the story. How many bell sounds can you find? There are 35 in all. Don't forget to include the bell sound in the title!

Full of baloney

Once upon a time, a girl named Bellamy was standing on her balcony eating a baloney sandwich. Bellamy's boy friend, Belvedere, was peering up at her from below.

"I've just returned from Belgium," he bellowed. "I've come to bring you a dinghy. I am tired of wading through the moat each time I want to see you. I can tie the dingy to the balcony with a piece of string," suggested Belvedere.

Bellamy was nodding as she stood wringing her hands.

"What if my father should find out I am meeting you alone before our wedding?" belted out Bellamy.

"Don't be a dingaling!" shouted Belvedere. "It was your father who was cheering for an early wedding. He would rather see me steering a dinghy than watch you feeding your belly on the balcony with baloney sandwiches!"

The Ding-dong Game

Ask your teacher, librarian, or parent to read "Full of Baloney" to your class or to a group of your friends. Each time you hear a ding, a ring, a ting, or a bell sound, you must stand up and sit down again. Those who miss a sound are out of the game. The last player to remain in the game wins the "ding-dong" award in the shape of a bell.

A time to be together

New Year's Day is a special day. It is like a birthday party for the new
year. People feel happy and excited. They want to share this feeling with
their families. Family members gather together to welcome the new year.
They sing songs, eat special foods, and remember the old year.
They remember the happy times they have spent together. They look
forward to the good times that the family will have in the year to come.
Family members wish one another a "Happy New Year."

New Year's calling

People also want to celebrate with their friends. Today, many friends get
together on New Year's Eve. In the olden days, people went "calling"
on New Year's Day.

Young men carried cards with their names printed on them. They left a calling card at each home they visited. Often, during a visit, they would have a sandwich and a drink with the women of the household. Then they went back out into the cold to travel to the next home.

By the end of the day, some men had visited more than one hundred women. This was something to boast about. And boast they did!
Some men told the newspapers how many homes they had visited. They hoped to set a record for visiting the most women. To these young men, calling became a contest!

Some women also competed with one another. They counted the number of cards they had received from their callers. They boasted to their friends about how popular they were!

Hogmanay

People around the world have different ways of sharing New Year with their friends. Some of these customs date back many years.

Long ago in Scotland, friends and neighbors called on one another after midnight on New Year's Eve. New Year's Eve was called *Hogmanay*. Visitors brought bread, cheese, and buns to the homes they visited. They wished their neighbors good health. In Scotland, people wished one another "Waes hael" in a language called *Gaelic*. This meant "Be well!" The visitors and hosts drank a sweet or spiced ale out of a "Waes hael" or *Wassail* bowl. Many English and Scottish people still drink a toast from a Wassail bowl on New Year's Eve.

First-footing

Visiting on Hogmanay was a tricky business. There was a special tradition in Scotland called *first-footing*. The first person to set foot inside another person's home after midnight was the *first-footer*.

Not just any first-footer was welcome. Some people believed that if their first visitor had blond or red hair, the family would have bad luck in the year to come. A tall, dark-haired visitor was believed to bring good luck. Sometimes, a dark-haired member of the family stood outside the home a few minutes before midnight. As soon as the clock struck midnight, the "visitor" quickly stepped inside. The family wanted to be certain that the first-footer was one who would bring good luck!

Many young men hurried to visit the homes of young women. If a young man was the first-footer to a woman's house, he received a kiss. Sometimes an old grandmother would play a prank. When the first-footer knocked on the door, she would answer it. The young man had hoped for a kiss from his sweetheart, not her grandmother!

A silent visit

A first-footer carried a piece of coal. This gift was added to the fire in the hearth of the home he visited. He put bread and salt on the kitchen table as a sign of friendship. He was given food and a drink in return for his presents. No one spoke when the first-footer was in the home. To do so was bad luck. The first-footer spoke only as he was leaving. He wished the family a very happy New Year.

What will the new year bring?

In many countries on New Year's Eve, people try to guess the future. In Scotland, people used to look at the color of the first-footer's hair. This told them if the next year would be lucky or not. Today, in some countries, people melt lead and pour a small amount of it into a cup of water. When the lead meets the water, it forms a shape. People look at the shape. They try to imagine what the shape can tell them about the future. The shape of a boat might mean they will go on a trip. The shape of a coin might mean they will receive money.

Seeing into the future

People have invented many ways of trying to see into the future. In the old days, young people looked in a mirror on New Year's Eve. They believed that they would see a reflection of both their own face and the face of the person they would marry.

Some people in England looked for objects that their feet had never touched. They took the objects outside, and each person stood on one. The people bowed nine times to the moon, and then they went to bed. Everyone hoped to dream of the person he or she would marry.

Sky signs

In Switzerland, some people believed that a bright red sky on New Year's Day meant that the year would have many storms. In the early days of North America, some people believed that it was good luck if the sun shone on New Year's Day. This meant that there would be enough fish and wild fowl to eat in the new year.

Wet or dry?

In Germany on New Year's Day, some people used to cut twelve onions in half. Each onion was named after a month of the year. The people put salt on each onion. If the salt on the January onion dissolved, the month would be wet. If the salt did not dissolve, the month would be dry. People believed that the weather of each month in the coming year could be predicted in this way.

What the animals predict

In Vietnam, people listen carefully on the first morning of the new year. When they hear a dog bark, they are happy. The dog will keep away burglars during the year to come. If they hear a rooster crow, the farmers will have bad crops. Roosters and chickens will eat the grain before it is planted. If they hear the buffalo bellow, the year will be full of hard work. Make up your own list of animals. Imagine what their sounds might mean. Then listen carefully for animals on New Year's morning.

Tie your fortune to a tree

In Japan, some people buy charms on New Year's Eve. These charms are fortunes or predictions written on folded pieces of paper. People read the fortunes to find out what the new year will bring. Sometimes, if they like what the fortune tells them, they tie the paper to a tree. They believe this will help the fortune come true.

What do you predict?

The new year holds many surprises. Make a list of the things that you think might happen next year. These guesses are called predictions. Someone may visit your family. You may go on a trip. You may go to a new school. You may visit one of your relatives. What do you predict? Keep your list. When the year is over, read the list again. See how many of your predictions came true.

21

Saint Sylvester's Day

Many European countries, such as France, Hungary, Switzerland, Belgium, Germany, and Austria, call December 31 *Saint Sylvester's Day*. Sylvester lived in Rome more than 1,500 years ago. He was the Pope. The Pope is the head of the Roman Catholic Church. On December 31, many people remember this good man. When they celebrate New Year's Eve, they are also celebrating St. Sylvester's Eve.

People celebrate St. Sylvester's Eve in many ways. In Germany, people feast on St. Sylvester's Eve. They eat a fish called carp. They call it St. Sylvester's Carp. They drink St. Sylvester's Punch. It is red wine with cinnamon in it. When the feast is over, people save a scale of the carp. They believe that the carp scale is a good-luck charm for the new year.

People go to church on St. Sylvester's Eve. They celebrate the time when St. Sylvester was the Pope. In some places in the countryside, people bring their cattle to the church. A priest blesses the cattle so they will be healthy in the year to come.

Will you be Sylvester?

In Belgium, Switzerland, and Germany, children leap out of bed as early as they can on December 31. Why do they do this? The last child out of bed is called "Sylvester." This child must pay a small fine to his or her brothers and sisters. What time do you usually get out of bed? What time do you think you would have to get out of bed on St. Sylvester's Day to avoid being Sylvester?

23

24

Costume parties

In some European countries, people dress up in costumes on New Year's Eve. They have parties with their friends. They dance, sing, and chat with one another. Sometimes they cannot tell which friend they are talking to!

How many different costumes can you see in this picture? Which is the funniest costume? Will you dress up on New Year's Eve? What costume will you wear? Will anyone be able to recognize you? At midnight, take off your mask. Now your friends will know they were talking to you!

New Year parades

New Year is a time for parades. In Greece, groups of people parade from home to home. They carry paper figures of apples, ships, and stars. Children receive coins and gifts. In Syria and Lebanon, children parade from door to door greeting their neighbors.

In Oberammergau, West Germany, the New Year parade takes two or three hours to pass by. The leader of the parade sings songs about the past year. The leader carries a long pole with a star at the top. The people in the parade wear colorful costumes. They dance to the music of a band.

Parades are fun

In Nepal, a small country between Tibet and India, there are four days of parades during the New Year festival. In Hong Kong and Taiwan, there are dragon and lion parades. In Morocco, there is a parade on the tenth day of the Muslim New Year. People dance as they parade. They carry lanterns on canes. Many dress up and wear masks.

In Thailand, there is a three-day New Year festival. On the second day of the festival, a woman is chosen to lead the parade. Green dragons, blue buffalos, elephants, and giants are favorite costumes. People march to the beat of drums and gongs.

The Tournament of Roses Parade

In the United States, New Year's Day is a day of football games. Almost one hundred years ago, people decorated their horse-drawn buggies and then traveled together in them to see sporting events. These were the first American New Year's Day parades. What a sight! Ever since those early days, there have been New Year's Day parades in the United States. One of the most famous is the Tournament of Roses Parade. The floats in the parade are decorated with flowers.

Keeping mum

Have you ever heard of mummers and mumming? Mummers dress in costumes. They parade down the streets, banging drums and blowing horns. They act out scenes from plays. Then they go from home to home. When the mummers are invited inside for food and a drink, their hosts try to guess who is behind each costume. The mummers do not speak. They keep ''mum.''

Mumming used to be a popular Christmas and New Year activity about one hundred and fifty years ago. The tradition of mumming is no longer carried out in most places. However, mumming parades are still held in Philadelphia and parts of Newfoundland on New Year's Day.

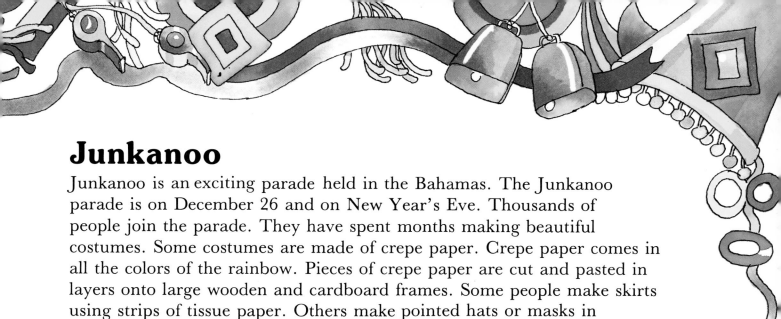

Junkanoo

Junkanoo is an exciting parade held in the Bahamas. The Junkanoo parade is on December 26 and on New Year's Eve. Thousands of people join the parade. They have spent months making beautiful costumes. Some costumes are made of crepe paper. Crepe paper comes in all the colors of the rainbow. Pieces of crepe paper are cut and pasted in layers onto large wooden and cardboard frames. Some people make skirts using strips of tissue paper. Others make pointed hats or masks in the shapes of bird heads or animal heads. At the end of the parade, prizes are awarded for the strangest or most beautiful costumes.

What's in a name?

No one knows for certain how the word Junkanoo came to be. Some people believe that Junkanoo comes from the French phrase, ''gens inconnus.'' ''Gens inconnus'' means ''unknown people.'' When people are wearing costumes, it is hard to recognize them. The Junkanoo paraders are unknown to their friends.

Some people believe that a famous hero called Johnny Canoe lived in the Bahamas. He wore a tall hat, tattered colorful clothes, and a mask. He appeared every year in December. People were so happy to see him, they danced and sang when he came. The celebration that took place when Johnny Canoe appeared became the Junkanoo festival and parade.

Can you Junkanoo?

Close your eyes and imagine yourself watching the Junkanoo parade. See the parade go by! Hear the cow bells, the whistles, the trumpets, and the drums. Hear the calypso and goombay songs. Sing along! See the people shaking, marching, and dancing. They will dance in the streets until the sun rises on a new day. Dance along! Pick out your favorite costume. Will it win the festival prize?

Have a parade

You and your friends can have your own parade. All you need is crepe or tissue paper, tape, cardboard, and plenty of imagination! Invent a name for your parade. Can you think of several interesting and funny reasons for choosing the name?

CRASH! BANG! BOOM! WHISTLE!

As you parade, make noise to welcome the new year. Many people used to think that noise frightened away evil spirits. They also believed that noise frightened away the old year and made room for the new year.

Collect pots and pans from the kitchen. Bang on them with wooden spoons. Tap on tin cans. Rattle a spoon in a glass. Ring cow bells, dinner bells, or sleigh bells. Ring the alarm on the alarm clock. Tie flowerpots on a string and strike these musical pots with a spoon.

Make a drum. Wrap brown paper tightly across the open end of a box or garbage can. Hit the paper with a stick or spoon.

Glasses, bottles, and jugs

Use glasses to make music. Pour water into several glasses so that the water in each glass is at a different level. Tap each glass with a spoon. Notice the different sounds that you hear. Play a New Year song!

Pour different amounts of water into several wine glasses. Wet your finger. Carefully run it around the rim of a glass. Do this several times until you hear a strange humming sound. Try each glass. Are the sounds different?

Fill bottles and jugs with water. Blow straight across the open top of each container. Toot in the new year!

Rattle in the new year

Make maracas. A maraca rattles! Cover one end of a toilet-paper roll or a tin can with paper or cardboard. Into the open end, put dry beans or peas, small nails, pebbles, paper clips, or raw rice. Cover the open end. Now rattle!

You can make gift noisemakers for your friends. Put candy and trinkets into a tube or can. Then wrap the tube or can in tissue paper. Tie the tissue with a ribbon and fringe the paper at each end.

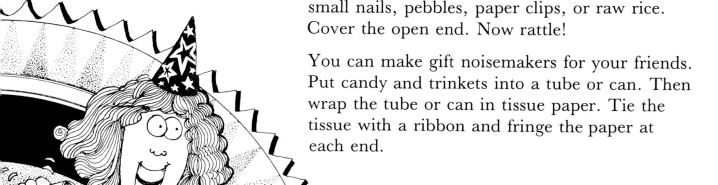

You can give these noisemakers to your friends at a New Year party. When your friends have finished rattling, they can enjoy the treats inside the maracas.

Make a pie-pan tambourine. Take two tinfoil pans. Put pebbles, beans, or raw rice inside one pan. Tape the other pan over the top of the first pan. Decorate the tambourine with tissue paper and streamers. Bang and shake your tambourine.

Whistle away the old year

Make a paper whistle. Cut two long, narrow strips of paper of the same size. Fold over one end of each strip. Hold the paper strips between the second and third finger in one hand, with the palm facing you. The folds in the paper lie side by side. Now, separate your fingers a little. Put your lips on the short flaps and blow hard. What a shriek!

Make a straw whistle. Take a paper or plastic straw and snip off a small piece. Flatten one end of the longer piece. Place the flattened end in your mouth and blow through the straw. Now, do the same with the short piece. Make straws of varied lengths and listen to the different noises you can make.

If you have no materials, celebrate the New Year by whistling, clapping your hands, stamping your feet, and slapping your knees. Use your voice. Sing, shout, hoot, yelp, yip, whoop, howl, shriek, squeal, and yowl. Make any noises you can. Welcome the new year!

Chinese New Year

The Chinese New Year is celebrated between mid-January and mid-February. It is the most important Chinese festival. It lasts for five days. Families are very busy before the festival. They settle arguments with friends. They prepare food for all visitors who will come to their homes during the festival. They clean their homes and put up signs and decorations.

On New Year's Day, gifts are exchanged. Children give one another oranges and candy. Parents wrap money in gold and red paper and give it to their children. There is a "money tree" in each home. Large pine and cypress tree branches are placed in a vase. They are then decorated with old coins and paper flowers.

Dancing in the streets

The Lion Dance begins on the third day of the New Year. It continues until the fifth day. Men dress in lion costumes and dance through the streets. The shopkeepers wrap money in red paper. The Chinese believe

that red is a lucky color. The shopkeepers hang this "lucky money" in high places. The dancers climb on top of one another. They form a human ladder in order to reach the money.

The Dragon Dance also takes place on the third day of the New Year. The head of the dragon is made of papier-mâché. The dragon's body is a long train of velvet, decorated with sparkles. One or two men hold the head of the dragon. Twelve men act as the dragon's legs. Families open the doors of their homes as the dragon passes. They welcome the good luck that the dragon brings.

Frightening out the old year

In the old days, people believed that explosions scared away Shan-sau. Shan-sau was the evil spirit who brought bad luck to the new year. People also believed that loud noises frightened the old year away. The streets are noisy on the day of the Dragon Dance. There are drums beating, people shouting, and firecrackers popping.

The Chinese horoscope

Buddha was a very great teacher. One day, he invited all the animals on earth to a meeting. Only twelve animals came. They arrived one by one.

Which animal are you?

The Chinese believe that each year is named after one of these twelve animals. Every twelve years the list begins again. Each animal is different from all the others. Each animal has different looks, different habits, and different ways of doing things. In the Chinese horoscope, the year of your birth is named after an animal. Read the following poem. Find the year of your birth. Some Chinese believe that you will have the same qualities as the animal of the year in which you were born.

Rats 1984, 1972, 1960
Rats are fair and Rats work hard.
They love to save their money.
They gossip about their friends so much
That no one calls them "honey."

Oxen 1985, 1973, 1961
Oxen are strong but stubborn, too.
They often lead the way.
Their talents are in arts and crafts,
And through writing, they have their say!

Tigers 1986, 1974, 1962
Tigers are brave as well as kind.
They like to flirt with danger.
They never seem to trust a soul,
Be it family, friend, or stranger.

Rabbits 1975, 1963, 1951
Rabbits need to feel secure,
Though they are bright and stable.
People trust their common sense.
They're calm and kind and able.

Dragons 1976, 1964, 1952
Dragons are good at politics.
They're flashy, bold, and loud.
They try hard to be their very best.
It's no wonder that they're proud!

Snakes 1977, 1965, 1953
Snakes look sharp and dress their best.
They're admired, rich, and wise.
They'll always climb to the very top.
If they fall, they will quickly rise.

Horses 1978, 1966, 1954

Horses work hardest of them all.
They'll do anything for a friend.
They're talented and popular,
But impatient to the end!

Rams 1979, 1967, 1955

Rams are always gifted souls.
Through art they'll earn their bread.
They work best when you least expect.
They'll always get ahead.

Monkeys 1980, 1968, 1956

Monkeys are funny as can be;
They're always playing tricks.
They're full of pranks and love new things,
But might put you in a fix.

Roosters 1981, 1969, 1957

Roosters hate to make mistakes.
They love to be the boss.
They tend to dream their time away,
But they're very seldom cross.

Dogs 1982, 1970, 1958

Dogs are faithful and make great friends.
They're sometimes very beautiful.
They can be stubborn and selfish, too,
But above all, they are dutiful!

Boars 1983, 1971, 1959

Boars are honest, brave, and proud,
And they will never bore you.
Boars love to learn and hate to fight.
They'll always stand up for you!

35

Tsao-Chun's report

Tsao-Chun is the name of the Chinese kitchen god. He watches over the kitchen all year. People work hard to keep him happy in the month before New Year. People believe that Tsao-Chun goes back to heaven at this time. Children make decorated paper chariots that carry the kitchen god to heaven. When he is in heaven, Tsao-Chun reports on each family. Everyone wants a good report.

Each home is cleaned and scrubbed. Walls are painted or whitewashed. The home is decorated. New Year messages are written in a beautiful script. They are attached to windows and doors. After all their hard work, people *still* don't trust Tsao-Chun to give a good report! They smear his picture with candy or honey. That way, he will say sweet things in heaven about the people he has visited.

What would Tsao-Chun say?

Doug and Kimberley decided to cook a feast for their parents. Things got a little out of hand! They had no idea that Tsao-Chun was on his round of kitchen reporting. He saw the mess. It was his duty to make a list of all the things that were out of place in this kitchen. What do you think was on his list?

Tsao-Chun had a soft heart, however. He felt that the children were very thoughtful to cook a dinner for their parents. What else do you think Tsao-Chun might have written in his report?

Facts on food

People believe that the color or taste of special foods will bring good luck and happiness in the coming year. They choose these special foods to eat at the New Year feast.

Thin buckwheat noodles called *soba* are served in Japanese homes. The long noodles are believed to bring long life to those who eat them. Hot soup is poured over the noodles to make a dish called *toshikoshi soba*. To bring good luck, children try to swallow one whole noodle without chewing it.

For the last meal of the old year, Chinese people prepare a feast of ten bowls of meat, ten bowls of vegetables, and ten cups of wine. The Chinese believe that ten is the perfect number.

Greek children receive a cake covered in almonds and walnuts. This "Saint Basil's cake" has a coin baked inside for a lucky child to find. Eating something sweet on New Year's Day is believed to bring a sweet year.

Many people eat red foods for a lucky year. They eat red peppers, tomatoes, cherries, and apples. Some people believe that pork is a good New Year meat. Because pigs root forward in the dirt, those who eat pork look forward to the coming year.

On the Jewish New Year's Day, some people slice apples and dip them into honey. They hope this will make the new year sweet.

It is a New Year custom in India to give friends and neighbors a lemon or lime for good luck. The fruit is placed in baskets outside the door of each home. When a basket is full, it means that the people in the home have many friends.

On New Year's Eve in Greece and Spain, there is a special food ceremony. At midnight, people pop a grape into their mouth each time the clock strikes. They pop twelve grapes for twelve months of good luck.

A New Year feast

The following recipes use lucky foods. What kind of year will each dish bring? What dish would you choose to serve? If you are planning to use the oven or stove to make some of these foods, be sure that a parent or older person is there to help you.

New Year's Noodles

Cook long noodles in boiling water. While the noodles cook, put a small amount of vegetable oil in a wok or big frying pan. Stir-fry strips of pork, tomato, and green and red pepper. Add salt and pepper. Serve the pork mixture on top of the noodles.

Lucky Lemon-lime Punch

Take a pitcher. Squeeze the juice from three lemons and three limes into it. Add ice and 750 mL (3 cups) of water. Add sugar and stir until the punch tastes sweet.

New Year's Honey Cake

625 mL (2 1/2 cups) flour
60 mL (1/4 cup) sugar
6 mL (1 1/4 teaspoon) baking powder
5 mL (1 teaspoon) cinnamon

2 eggs
250 mL (1 cup) liquid honey
125 mL (1/2 cup) vegetable oil
almonds and red candied cherries

1. Grease a 23 x 33 cm (9'' x 12'') baking dish.
2. Mix flour, sugar, baking powder, and cinnamon in a large bowl.
3. Stir with fork.
4. Whisk eggs in another mixing bowl.
5. Add honey and oil to eggs, then stir.
6. Slowly stir dry mixture into egg mixture until blended. Stir in almonds.
7. Pour mixture into pan and decorate with red candied cherries.
8. Bake for 25 to 30 minutes in a pre-heated 180°C (350°F) oven.

If your New Year's Honey Cake is a flop, don't put it in the garbage. In England, there is a New Year custom called "breaking the cake." Children throw cakes against a wall or a door. Breaking a cake brings good luck, but only at New Year!

Japanese New Year

Early in December, people in Japan begin to prepare for the New Year holiday. They buy special food. They make lucky decorations using pine, bamboo, and rope. The rope reminds the Japanese people of the Sun Goddess.

The story of the Sun Goddess

One day, the Sun Goddess hid in a large cave. Suddenly, the world went dark. The other gods and goddesses wanted the sun to shine. They had to find a way to get the Sun Goddess out of the cave! They thought of a plan. They danced and sang outside the cave. Finally, the Sun Goddess poked her head out so she too could enjoy the party. Quickly, the gods and goddesses pulled her out of the cave. They placed rope over the entrance so the Sun Goddess could not hide again. The world was no longer dark during the day! This is why rope is used as a decoration during the New Year season. The Japanese want the new year to be bright.

Good-bye to the old

The Japanese send New Year cards to their friends. Many people visit temples and shrines to pray to the gods for a good year. There are "forgetting-year" parties. People say good-bye to the old year. They forgive their friends for any disagreements they have had.

Hello to the new

December 31 is the "Grand Last Day" of the year. On this day, homes are cleaned and stores are closed. In the evening, the bells ring. Some Japanese people believe that every person has 108 troubles. The bells ring 108 times to chase away the 108 troubles. When midnight arrives, everyone says, "*Akemashite omedeto gozaimasu.*" This means "Congratulations, the New Year has come."

A day of fun

In Japan, New Year's Day is like a birthday party. Everyone celebrates. People dress in colorful kimonos. They eat a special breakfast and open their New Year cards. Children receive *otoshidamas* from their parents and other adults. These are small packages with money inside. Some people visit their friends and family. Others travel up to the mountains for a skiing holiday. New Year's Day is a day to have fun.

Japanese New Year games

Hanetsuki

In Japan, New Year's Day is a time to play games. Children fly kites and spin tops. They get out their new paddles. The paddles are used to play *Hanetsuki*. This game is like badminton. The children use their paddles to hit a small ball of cork. Feathers are attached to the cork. Players try to keep the ball flying through the air.

Karuta

You may like to try this game. On New Year's Day, Japanese children take cards and write verses of famous poems on them. They cut the cards in half. The bottom halves of the cards are mixed together and placed in a pile. One player keeps the top halves. He or she reads the beginning of a poem from the top half of a card. The other players scramble to search through the pile for the card with the rest of the poem.

Kakizome

On January 2, Japanese children write a poem or a proverb on a long piece of paper. This special writing is called *Kakizome*. Japanese writing is quite beautiful. Each word looks like a picture.

Can you write a special New Year's Day poem? Do it in your best printing or writing style. Use a pen, a pencil, or a paintbrush. Instead of words, try using little pictures to tell a story. See if your friends can read your New Year message.

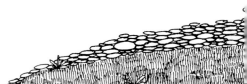

Fuku Wari

Another Japanese New Year's Day game is called *Fuku Wari*. Children take a large piece of paper. They draw the outline of a head on it. They color in the hair. They tape the outline to a door or wall. Then they take another large piece of paper. They draw eyes, eyebrows, eyelashes, ears, a nose, and a smiling mouth on the paper. All these drawings are cut out.

Now the fun begins! Each cutout has a pin or a piece of tape attached to it. A child is given a cutout, is blindfolded, and must find the way to the outline of the face. The child must then try to pin or tape the cutout to the right place on the face. Do you know a game similar to this one? Of course! It is called Pin the Tail on the Donkey.

Diwali

The people who believe in the Hindu religion in India have a New Year celebration four times every year. There is a New Year to welcome each of the four seasons. Diwali is one of the most popular New Year festivals. It is a five-day festival at the beginning of autumn. Several days before Diwali starts, people begin their preparations. They clean their homes and their shops and decorate their doorways. They take colorful powders and make patterns on their doorsteps.

Festival of Lights

Diwali is called the Festival of Lights. On the evening before Diwali begins, children light their *dipas*. These are small clay lamps. The dipas are placed on the flat roofs of homes, on window ledges, and along the paths that lead to each home. One family may have hundreds or even thousands of these lamps! The lamps will burn for the five days of the festival.

Why are the lamps so important? The Hindu goddess of good luck visits people's homes during Diwali. She will visit only the homes that are brightly lit. She brings new clothes and toys for the children.

Young girls float their dipas across rivers and lakes. If the dipa is still lit when it reaches the far side, it is believed that the girl and her family will have good luck in the new year.

The first day of Diwali is the "New Year of Business." Business people return the money they owe. Machinery, cars, and trucks are blessed and decorated with flowers and palm leaves. People want the machinery to run well in the new year.

On another day of Diwali, brothers and sisters have a special ceremony. They promise that they will continue to love one another and be good friends.

Diwali is a time for dances, songs, and fireworks. It is a time for feasts, presents, and light. Diwali is a wonderful celebration.

Rosh Hashanah

Rosh Hashanah is the Jewish New Year. It is at the end of the summer or the beginning of the autumn. It is the first day of the first month of the Jewish calendar. *Rosh* means ''head'' or ''beginning.'' *Hashanah* means ''of the year.''

On the evening before Rosh Hashanah, people recite a blessing, called *Kiddush*, over wine. After the prayer there is a special meal. Everyone eats a piece of egg bread, called *challah*. The challah looks like a crown. This shape reminds people that God is the king of heaven. The challah is round and smooth. People hope the new year will run smoothly.

L'shanah Tovah

On the day of Rosh Hashanah, the family goes to the synagogue. A synagogue is a place of worship. A *shofar* is blown during the service. The shofar is a ram's horn. Long ago, it was blown to call people together in times of danger. Now, it reminds people that they must always help one another. At the synagogue, people wish their family and friends *L'shanah Tovah* or "Good New Year."

Wishes for a good New Year

There is a Jewish belief that at New Year, God writes a description of what each person's year will be like. God writes this in a big book. People send cards to one another with the wish that God will write a good new year for them in the book. People also think about the good times they have had in the past year.

A time to remember

New Year's Day is a time for reminiscing. To reminisce means to talk about past times. It is fun to share old memories and experiences. Sometimes people forget how special they are to one another. Reminiscing is a good way to bring people together.

Start a family diary

Write down all the important things that have happened to your family in the past week. For example, "Lisa lost her tooth on Wednesday," or "Mother started her new job on Monday." Describe how each family member felt about the events of the week. The next week, another member of your family takes a turn. Read your diary on New Year's Day. What kind of year has your family had? You could make a list of all the best things that have happened to you in the past year. Finish the diary with this list.

New Year words

Try to use all these words in your own New Year story.

Chinese dragon

dipa

mask

costume

mummers

money tree

calendar

Janus

Fuku Wari

calling cards

balloons

party hat

streamers

whistle

confetti

challah

noodles

St. Basil's cake

carp

Wassail bowl

bells

new moon

shofar

midnight

Did you know?

Did you know that in northern Portugal, children sing *janeiros* on New Year's Day? They sing these old songs as they walk from home to home. This is believed to bring good luck. The children are given treats and coins.

Did you know that New Year in Iran is called No-Ruz? No-Ruz means the new day. No-Ruz is the first day of spring and the first day of the new year. Families gather on New Year's Eve. They watch for special things to happen at midnight. The goldfish stands still in its bowl. An orange spins in a pot of water. An egg trembles when the New Year begins. People kiss each other and say, "May you live for a hundred years."

Did you know that in Siam, which is now Thailand, each year had a special name? On New Year's Day, the king had a special ceremony and gave a new name to the new year.

Did you know that at New Year in Bolivia, families hang little dolls outside their homes? The dolls are made of wood or straw. The dolls bring good luck.

Did you know that people in Denmark used to save all their old pots, pans, and broken dishes? On New Year's Eve, they threw them at the doors of the homes where their friends lived. It was a good sign to have a large heap of broken dishes outside your door. It meant that you had many friends!

Did you know that in Laos, people go to a temple on the first day of the new year? The temple courtyard is decorated with flags and flowers. If two friends make a sand mound in the courtyard, they will remain good friends through the year. People throw water at one another. They want to wash away the old year.

Did you know that on New Year's Day in Ecuador, people stuff old clothing with straw to make a scarecrow? This scarecrow is Old Year. Old Year sits in a chair in front of the family's home. The parents and children write a list of all the family's faults. They place this list in the lap of Old Year. Then Old Year and the list of faults are burned. Good-bye, Old Year. Hello, New Year!

Did you know that Romanians believed that farm animals talked on New Year's Day? No one wanted to hear the animals talk, though. It was believed to bring bad luck.

Did you know that in Bangladesh, New Year comes in April? Flowers decorate the streets. People put colored powder on their doorsteps to welcome the year. They wear red and yellow clothes because red and yellow are the colors of spring.

Did you know that on New Year's Eve in Syria and Lebanon, children travel from home to home? They receive coins and candy. Families put a bowl of water and a dish of wheat outside their homes. These are for the youngest camel. A long time ago, the youngest camel brought gifts to Jesus at Christmastime.

Did you know that in Nepal, New Year's Day is called Nava Barsa? Nava Barsa means "to leave the past."

Did you know that Armenian women celebrate New Year by making special bread? The bread is pressed or kneaded. The bread has luck for the new year kneaded right into it!

New Year's resolutions

Celebrating the New Year with parades, costumes, and parties is fun for everyone. For many people, New Year's Day is also a time for making decisions. People decide how they can make their new year better than the old one. This story is about a girl who makes an important decision on New Year's Day.

Messy Allison cleans up

It was the beginning of a brand-new year. Allison wanted to make a New Year's resolution. Her grandmother had told her that a New Year's resolution is a decision that people make at the beginning of the year. It can be a decision to try harder at something or to break a bad habit.

Allison thought to herself, "I have so many bad habits. I lose my mittens on the way to school, and sometimes I'm not as nice to my brother as I should be. But my worst habit is messiness. I guess that's why people call me Messy Allison."

Allison looked around her bedroom. Clothes were lying everywhere. Her stuffed animals were scattered across the floor. Socks and sweaters hung out of the dresser drawers. "What a mess!" she thought.

Allison decided to make her New Year's resolution. "I'm going to be neat for a whole year. No more Messy Allison. I'm going to remember to pick up my clothes and put away my toys."

Allison smiled happily. It felt good to make a New Year's resolution! But then she took another look at her messy room. Her bed was unmade. It was covered with books and toys. Over in the corner, the glass eyes of her stuffed elephant, Jojo, winked sadly.

"It's going to be awfully hard to keep my New Year's resolution for a whole year," Allison sighed. "Maybe I should just try to be neat for half the year. I can start right now by cleaning up this room."

Allison started picking up her stuffed animals and putting them back on the shelves where they belonged. "This is going to be a big job. Once this room is neat, it's going to be very hard to keep it neat."

Allison frowned and started to clear the books off her bed. "I don't know if I can promise to be neat for half the year. Maybe I should try to be neat for just one day!"

Allison started to smile again. She hugged Jojo and told him, "Now, that's a New Year's resolution I know I can keep."

Auld Lang Syne

In many countries, people sing a special song at the stroke of midnight on New Year's Eve. It is called ''Auld Lang Syne.'' This means ''for old time's sake.'' This song is about remembering your friends and the good times you have had with them.

Should auld acquaintance be forgot
And never brought to mind?
Should auld acquaintance be forgot,
And days of auld lang syne!

Chorus
For auld lang syne, my dear,
For auld lang syne,
We'll take a cup of kindness yet
For auld lang syne.

Looking forward

People around the world celebrate New Year at different times. They celebrate in different ways. But everyone agrees that New Year is a time of joy. Everyone looks forward to a new year full of good things.

Happy New Year to you!

Index

567890LB Printed in the USA 987654